14/24 mw

7

BLOOD / SUGAR

BLOOD/SUGAR

James Byrne

PUBLICATIONS

2009

Published by Arc Publications
Nanholme Mill, Shaw Wood Road
Todmorden OL14 6DA, UK
www.arcpublications.co.uk

Copyright © James Byrne 2009
Design by Tony Ward
Printed in Great Britain by the
MPG Books Group, Bodmin and King's Lynn

978 1906570 28 6 pbk
978 1906570 29 3 hbk

ACKNOWLEDGEMENTS:

The author is grateful to the editors of the following magazines and anthologies in which some of these poems, or versions of these poems, first appeared: *Ambit, Cimarron Review, The Delinquent, Fulcrum, Golden Boat, Jacket, The Manhattan Review, Openned (Anthology vol.1), Oxfam (CD: Life Lines 2), Poetry Review, Poetry Wales, Salt Magazine, Times Online* and *Vair*.

A selection of the poems in this book were first published in *The Vanishing House (Kuca koja iscezava)* by Treci Trg in 2009.

The front cover is an overpainted photograph, '18.1.89', by Gerhard Richter. The author is grateful to Gerhard Richter for granting permission to republish his artwork.

Thanks to John Wedgwood Clarke, John Kinsella and Sandeep Parmar for reading different versions of this manuscript. Additionally, thanks to the Arts Council England for giving the author a grant to complete this book.

Supported by
ARTS COUNCIL
ENGLAND

Editor for the UK and Ireland: John W. Clarke

for my mother
Mary Shuttle

Contents

Recovery

Let me imagine you coming home
from the dark, between body and mind,

making evidence of yourself
the way a tree waves up from its shadow.

There are dinner-halls you have silenced
with a single spark of wit,

there are men you have governed
through pure scent, pure posture.

Now for your most difficult trick:
to restart a life that ends by turning into gold.

In September (the month that tends to all others)
let me be able to conjure your best side,

to have some kind of grip on the intactness
of living, the way mirrors do.

Apprentice Work

i.m. Peter Redgrove

The lithic who makes a pal in death
teaches me not to die so slowly.
'Many ways to become lineal' he says,
'to write The Sounding Book'.

Everything close as a finger thimble;
a lock of hair from Proserpine,
the tropics in Technicolor,
drumcliff tapped by a solitary cloud.

You lifted a finger over Gogol,
Little Russia droned bee-like.
And when they fired you up
Uhland took you in his colossal lung.

*

I've arrived late, apprentice imp,
to where you tripped out on yoga visions
and saw the 22,000 year origins of art
insetted by a single flint;
to the Gale Chambers of the Vast Nose,
Cornish galleons tucked under the ocean like rain.

Who's to decide between glass economies
or the drowsy pulp of the sea?
It ties the forensic squad in knots –

the way groundswell fattens
from a single rock, remakes itself
into delicate gemstone.

*

These days The Book of Thresholds
fits firm for a pillow,
it wakes me with an empire's relish.

No identity preference, no thumb guide.
Only scent variations,
each murmurous, each perennial.

The footnotes appear Pythagorean
cupid seminaries/vanity carnivals
vs. GIGANTIC LABOUR.

No monument decision –
nothing on the slumberous reek
of a salmon polished by the sun.

*

We apprentice poets need an innovator,
'verbal haemoglobin', not a casket key.
I repeat the only rule you knew as mantra:

everything is invitation.

Air Terminals

for Sandeep

> '...I dreamed
> of a page in a book containing the word bird and I
> entered bird.'
>> Anne Carson, 'Gnosticism I'

Reading how Mansfield claims the word *air*
is to live in it.

Pure scheme vs. science anxiety.

Not the *duck of a boy* emphatic
nor the rich-leaning Rosemary,

more a chance to inhabit
adrenal pressure –
six hours of braided sky
pushed through cloud braille.

*

How to steady up when all at once
air batches you out to crash phobias,

night after night,
wing tensions grazing your head?

*

Small curve of trust in a child's joy at architecture.

At the terrorist check
threshold and counter-threshold –

a sparrow's fear of total sunlight,
a studious approach to Boeing assemblies.

*

Carefully your ration array of clothes
checked in tight folds   touches

and is how air means,

clipped around the roots of a hand

as you look back gesturing –
once   twice   finally.

*

Air as the steadying of addiction:
how to breathe as the shadow dips?

Air-guides to breakers at the logic gate
the perfect crime, always getting away.

Evidences in landing vapour –
the movement of my hand on your back that says

'go'.

*

The route I take I take on foot,
afraid and tenderly loyal.

At the ventilation tunnel
the smooth saturation of air vocals,
every tenor, decorous.

Your flaunting of altitude
is strictly west-hugging.

How the difference tells?

There was a cold bitter taste in the air
and the new-lighted lamps looked sad.

Days of 1973

'The chambers of his heart filling with faces.
Mine. Yours. A stranger trails around a corner.
Fuming echoes circle over a pair who argue
In some fiery tongue....A conversation
I broke off some years ago drifts up...'
                    J. D. McClatchy, 'From the Balcony',

'Fear was my father, Father Fear'.
                    Theodore Roethke 'The Lost Son'

I'll tell you, but not here.

*

To walk in tall shadows of the forest
is to invite further shadows.

The light astonishes from every exit-point.

*

Where the garden adjoins the house
by the crooked trunk of a Box Elder –
a father's priestly assurance...

If I've learnt anything since your mother...
man's lot is the muddied field, or no field.

*

Through the Elder's pinnate a crash of sun
parleys your temples –

the samara wings sigh,
a dense, calculated sigh.

*

For twenty years the abysm expanded, hard time
snared a decade...

'The kettle yearns for the mountain / The soap for the sea'

*

Your eyes are solemnised,
a colder blue.

On history they come and go.

But the mind – cunning enough to *act* on love –
audits and impels history,
mosses every stone.

*

I left the house with my own stare daggering your spine.

(...My brother and I hid knives under our shorts in the court lobby.

We were trained for the script.

To get off wrist-slapped was 'No Access'.)

*

In his shed study,
a simple swinging wire in the air turns to metronome…

…What happened during the Christmas of 1973…?

…There's a picture of my mother – cross-legged, all bones,
shrunken to her wits.

*

(…)*We was less than your age.* (…) *Hard to relive now.* (…)

(…) *She could temper the Saints, y'know.*

*

A decided jury-master,
the allegations stood –

                    Children for alcohol.
                    A cruiserweight finesse….

We rolled down the stairs – she and I –
three weeks from birth.

What if I was born then and what for
in our vanishing house?

*

This *is* access –
we are a mismatched couple tethered by blood.

*

His head is peppery and veined like marble,
something solid to look at,
yet doubling up as breakable.

*

If I break now
I am locked in for life.

*

(The notebook is fluent as the tongue.

I keep a photograph of my grandmother
on which reads a quote from Lowell's *History*
You were [his] *airhole.* '73.)

*

To equate such instances with all men fetches strength:

When men happen together
there's always some kind of tremoring business.

*

Cheap getaway, he fumbles with the door –
a side-glimpsed grin icteric with victory.

*

If it cannot be translated as it was...
a 'version' empowers me:

> *Pain is inevitable...*
> (how we clown after it)

> *Suffering is optional*
> (the first rule of confession).

*

In attic rooms of my father's house
I am everywhere and shushed quiet.

The smiles on the faces of blanched photographs
are proud and importedly Irish.

*

My grandmother's face
resumes in my face and
feeds the ghost between us.

*

There's more where that came from…

(I tore the cheque to shreds,
scattered it on your lawn.
It flew through the air
and held like confetti.

*

What it is…

    …like a kind of falling…

     I have failed you with my life.

Sestina for R
(with repetitions of two lines by Edna St Vincent Millay)

Dawn and again your voice cracks
like a vessel too thin for certain
vibrations. Demisting the window,
you rock gently from side-to-side,
your hand waving with a rhythm
that holds you to it as if by a drug.

Your doctor prescribes the same drug
on every visit, widening the cracks
in your downcast face. Deadly rhythm.
If treatment and health go side-by-side,
untreatable is your face at the window.
You're the same sunk vessel, for certain.

Like a vessel too thin for certain
vibrations, you re-alight in '91: a drug
binge at The Brain. Memory's window
props open, reconfiguring wisecracks
from the promo video. On the outside
you were a zeitgeister, the rhythm

of the club – the core of its rhythm.
What plans you had. Fame, for certain.
But the pilled-up crew at your side
guided a thin vessel. Love was the drug
fooled by its addiction. The cracks
widen in your profile at the window.

Who are you waiting for at the window?
The streetlamps click off to the rhythm
of a lit horizon. Chimney cracks
proffer terraced light to a certain
vibration, until the light, like a drug,
fires the body, flush full on the side

of your face (as if warmed from inside).
This is your life at the window.
Fear-hogged, shocked quiet by drug
after drug. Frail now, less of rhythm,
like a vessel too thin for certain
vibrations. Furrowed are the cracks.

Outside, traffic cargoes to a rhythm.
You hear a ghost sonata tap the window.
I listen in closely until your voice cracks.

A Private Garden

Early to rise for knowledge of the garden – for the fringe of a
    gossamer hammocking.
I watched the painful sum of its catch and knew the eeriness of
    death for the first time.
The spider trapezed his web, a thin ball of coal discovering its
    prey in filigrees of ash.
His victim, trapped in the jewel case, huddled appallingly for
    its life. A sudden drop
in the breeze and the kill was fished clean. Books have never
    taught me these things.

    *

Seated between the knuckled limbs of the tree house, I spied
    on a swarm of wasps
nuzzling at apples; their glassy colour-code and spoiling tails
    cranked with venom –
emblematic fire. In France, later that year, my mother
    broomed a nest and was fanged
by an army of them. A quickly pumped prescription pulled
    her back from an inch of life.
Full of the feast, a wasp landed on my hand and looked at me
    like a god, perfectly evil.

    *

For what seemed an era, I clutched at the giant slab to win
    one look under its shadow.
With a gravelly belch the stone pulled loose and revealed to
    me its secret archive –
the dark unendingness of a disused well. Peering in, I conjured
    the anaemical fix
of my father's stare and shouted down until my face burnt
    red: *This is my garden!*
There was music then. The chambered echoes passed through
    me to their reunions.

Widowed / Unwidowed

for Penelope Shuttle

I

Webwork hangs in fistfuls along the ferry dock

In blue diamond cold
it breaks
at the turning keel

> Niche of frost
> rumour of frost

> The wave stuns
> before it arrives

Across the Roseland peninsula
ghost lobbies make company
from window dressage

> Willowy sympathies at tearooms
> teeth in the wicker of a vacant chair

From Church Street to Arwenack Street
to the swivelling flap of a shop sign
thirty years recalled –

a yard of blue and leathery Shakespeares
the microwave ping of hammered-in typewriters
a Christmas tree hugged home from Harvey's

At night memory reconstitutes
a voice like solid blood –

The pillow turns on itself

The orchard owl
blots all sound
but its own sound

This is the year of the wasp
of apples sung to the core

II

Everything that comes from the sea
returns to the sea –

Ash of a life
The burnished pebble
The starfish in its marzipan coat

In libraries of pearly blown dust
through perfect darkness
and the echolalia of eight rivers –

I never went to University…
He was my University

Widowed / Unwidowed

Grief is *there* and *there*

A neighbour holds up a white orchid
with supreme inelegance
scaly-faced
shy as a child

'If there's *anything* I can do…'

The room is overbrim with bright water

The heart deals its pendants

Two Phonecalls at 4 am

'the world is places where he will not go'
                    John Berryman, *Dream Songs 65*

Little terrors in them,

small as a seed at first,
        soon a lion's head.

Lacking the mirror-work of Cocteau's *Orphée*
or the white throat of a Busoni sonata,

mismouths become crosscuts,

        the blue-black spell:
                garlic in the roses.

We offer anecdotes:

        Li Po drunk on Saki.
        Li Po bent mad over books.
        Li Po remade as a lithical martyr by Deng Xiaoping.

The voice through the black wire counterclaims that plans for a
        statue in Dresden
were recently disapproved on the grounds that the accompanying
        plaque was to state:

                            THE DEAD ARE SORE FOR REVENGE

Phonecalls cut the crowd.
A sympathetic ear smothers like a shot.
The response lies on the tongue like a cube of sugar.

It is the pip in our own voice that terrifies:
                    the voice of the sweetening epic.

From the Sky Parlour

'Men grow old, pearls grow yellow: there is no cure for it.'
Chinese proverb

The jewellery box,
      its cypress-wood exterior
            lacquered and cracked.

Inside
      the recherché –
                  our filigree of '82
                        the year we dartled above its casket.

I carry it now, as I always have,

                  novice erotologist   schoolboy thief,

he who picked the ring-locks of felt balconies,
who cooped a wreath of corundum

                        for months a secret necklace.

In turns, we played MOTHER,
      pranced for stickpins, tiaras –

                        our finest burlesques –

                        beau monde   grande dame   coquette.

With a row of button pearls,

                  unknowing   incurable,

I held the clasp around your neck,

     took grip   fastened.

Dowry for an Aerophobic

for Sandeep

Cymophane.
Silvering mineral.
The cat's-eye winks
from its luteous coat.

Vitreous, though resolute,
its kindly glamour
kin-quartz,
kin-tourmaline,

though a purer mix –
history pinioned,
no bigger than an eyeball.

Between flights and cities,
beyond the laps of mothers
and the tactical silence of old men,

its deep veins sparkle –
my fingertips inch out
while yours smooth
over the dark green trussing.

Close up,
the borosilicate twinkles,
fire-scented,
peppery beneath the sheen,

each striation coils back
to a hoard of riches –
Azilian ruby, liquid fossil, beryllium.

(It's enough to pearl a lithologist's pupil.)

Notice how –
in the flat of your palm –
electricity stirs

clockwise.

Counter-clockwise.

Speed Date (20th December 1970)

The signalling gift – a miniature Bushmills –
loosened from the rope of an espadrille.

She downs it in a gulp and winces –
the sting fires up like a sickness.

He spreads his legs, as if for a dance.
His superego draws new coordinates.

She sizes him according to rank and faculty.
As if their lives were the fate of a country.

Marry me. And in the flashing pause
the *Yes* in her mind intones a world.

Dousing the bright berg of an oil lamp
his shadow casts a gargantuan cage.

The kiss means nothing it understands.
It marks a map that outwits their age.

Serapis from a Postcard

for Zouzi Chebbi Mohamed Hasesen

Inventor-cool that Ptolemy –

smoothed down via dream-dictation,
he discovered the beard of Serapis,
and made dynastic the perfect lie.

Led to the unknown   by the unknown,
(from Macedon to Alexandria)

for your face on this postcard, Mohamed,
Goddio's magnetometer flashed green –

from the humming cave of a shiphead,
a four-month stint in the Grand Palais.

   *

To Google –

Serapis the amalgamator,
the ghost-bearded messiah,

part-western bull   part son of Geb,
a Jesus decoy agent.

From the ruins of the Daughter Library,
to the Yorkshire garrisons,

brushed / rebrushed
the bunko of his rock face.

*

Zouzi,

because the conclusiveness of one entity
is so crucial, so believed,

it carried Serapis from Alexandria
through Rome   to the Bishops of Christ,

to these glassy banks of Petrovaradin –

where you are God of Fertility,
God of the White River –

Half-hierophant,
        half-*king of the deep.*

The Buddhas of Bamiyan

...it is characteristic of matter to suffer action, i.e. to be moved;
but to move, i.e. to act, belongs to a different power.
Aristotle, *On Generation and Corruption, Book II*

The iconoclast, the mob that destroys a work of art is mob
because it fails to disassociate the work from a separate sig-
nificance.
Ezra Pound, *Guide to Kulchur*

Dust mocks the starched empty tombs at Bamiyan.

From the seventh century
to the 'War on Terror',
(bar a moment of confusion from Mahmud of Ghazni)
Salsal and Shamama remained unscathed –
shoehorned in the valley.

'Unholy', according to Sharia,
the rarest knuckle of sandstone along the Silk Road
dynamited to a niche-mark.

*

But belief is not always destroyed by action.

'What if...', says Dr. Tarzi,
'what if the Buddha's eye is still upstaring?'

*

Day after day, in red mud,
Dr. Tarzi – the 'Indiana Jones of Afghan Archaeology' –

adds toil to the bruise of a dream
he has suffered to stage since 1969 –
a 1,000ft. Buddha brushed from rubble.

*

'The death, even the disappearance, of something holy
is unreal to me'
says the tour guide,
a local Hazara, trained by Tarzi, who,
when the Taliban torched the villages around Kush Mountain,
had to bury all the men in his family.

*

The Buddhas of Bamiyan were larger than three football fields.
Roughly the same size as Ground Zero.

To destroy them requires a 'different power'.
A 'different faith'.

*

But belief suffers by action
and non-action.

For the believer and the image-breaker
loaded die –
vertigo and ultimatum.

This unpriceable loot,
(if it were priced and sold by the Taliban in 2001)
could have crowned any museum in the world;
could have fed every rampart,
every tower
along the Silk Road.

*

Massacre of history,
massacre of power –

by selling the Buddhas of Bamiyan
the Taliban might have housed enough ammunition
to condemn a rattle of quiet thunder from Zeus.

*

What keeps a man digging half his life?

It is said that for every one year of peace in the world
there are over four hundred years of war.

A King's Faith

after Cavafy's 'Manuel Commenus'

Such servants to certainty
these paid astrologers.
For kings, they augured faith
as a golden apple.

Faith, in how Kyr Manuel
one dreary September,
gives every crumb of the lording melancholy
from his cells
to a god who, like memory,
accomplishes nothing.

*

Untaxable in his monastic robes,
neither emperor nor king,
so quick to assume the incantatory monk.

In the depths of such dreaming,
Manuel sails the Aegean
to garden enfolds, ecclesiastical vines.

In his robe, a map of Byzantium.
His amulet: a pouch of gold.

Chess in Kirkuk

for Fadhil Al-Azzawi

'Two men tossing a coin, one keeping a castle'
Ezra Pound, 'Provincia Deserta'

In the Café Atlas, you furlonged over countless games of chess
with a signature move: checkmate, X'ings of bishop and queen.
Victorious, to be prized as a prisoner, while those you conquered
were laurelled with limousines and castles, the new ministers
of the slaughterhouse had you wearing old shoes from the dead
who had no time to put on their shoes when the guards burst in.

A thirty-year exile, honing your skill as chessmaster and prophet.
In Leipzig, you saw Saddam bare his polished teeth like Dracula.
In Paris, a mirror returned the blooded forehead of Al-Mutanabbi.
You saw Iraq's future torturers flogging their backs for bread
and wished them a square meal and a hex against the atom bomb.

Arriving into giant shafts of sunlight along the Turkish strait,
you remembered those who traded their poetry for propaganda;
not as turncoats; but simply chessmates flexing pawns for victory.

Nightnurse

for Hafiz Kheir & Al-Saddiq Al-Raddi

In Khartoum friends and relatives of the mentally ill are encouraged to stay with patients, especially during the night when staff shortages are at their highest.

The chart declares 'LOW RISK RELAPSE'
though scraps of sound interference

jam the brain, the nervous system fuse-lit,
the hissings of a father dead for three decades.

The volunteer nurses click away and the night porter
lets you in with a nod of gratitude.

For three months you have entered the blue ward
at Umdurman while your country shifted in ash.

This is what friendship is: to walk into a bare cell
with the sky on your back and a superabundance of gravity.

To arrive at the gates of the Al-Tahji Al-Mahi
armed with a copy of Adonis and a carton of cigarettes.

All through the night, war is glossed over. You replace it
with a world that rewards with luck and superstition,

where fruit falls freely along the banks of the White Nile
and friends grow old like rivers.

Sanchez de Aldama

Two Divorces

Stepping onto a train bound for Juarez,
she fills the carriage with her bitter scent:
Sevillian citrus. Its salacious oil, pungent,
deluxe: the kind that demands attention.
She takes a window seat and stares out:
her face fully-trained, tanned as a violin.
Fifteen miles away, I drive to meet her,
divorce papers plumping the glove-box
and a wedding stone in my right hand.
Soon she'll hook herself over my knees
and we'll lay claim to an honest life
until punished by the logic of the Gods.

Mérida

With a fifty-kilo barrel load of llello
and pickups crammed with Colt ARs,
we cross at Ahcanul from the gulf port.
Mérida: five-hilled city where the Spanish
autopsied the on-dead during caste war.
Here my grandmother knew her marriage
by counting the red feathers in a quetzal:
seven years quarantined to a muzzy drunk.
Where her house stood a sea hag sings
to the sun priest of Coba: *Come is the quetzal.*
Come is the bluebird. The sound of her voice
crackles in heat like the skin of a cochinita.

La Blanca Sabana

No doubt Juan Brea's body still rolls
on the floor of the sea. How cruel life is!
In the chanted spells of the brujas
he returns, beginning with a scream,
only to die out suddenly. Poor criminal,
his life had been hanging by its tail.
But, scoundrel that he was, it stands up
that every man deserves a white sheet,
a good heap of soil and faithful lament.
Juan Brea, the reeds are oxygenic but fail you,
as you failed in life and as I have failed you
with a bullet that stuck at tremendous speed.

Coda

What an end: a hole through the pump!
No devil's dice, no wand or antiseptic;
just the radio instinct of sirens wailing.
Snitchers? Any card from the pack.
In this job loyalty is a left-handed form
of confidence. The choice is made simple:
rat or be damned and if you haven't earned
enough time behind doors, or kept schtum
after a jinx, then you're a nothing but a crick
in the system. There is no green ending.
I gave my consent as someone born wicked,
with a nastiness that grows on from itself.

14th April 1930

En-route to the Pantheon,
weighing 300 grams more
than the average brain,

Mayakovsky's

unvenomned,
absolutely quiet.

Death-handled,
nowhere left to penetrate –

no red-syndicate idea like a mountain chain,
no gap for lovelessness, no 'lasting wounds'.

The state surgeons put down their scalpels
and package you off to the Institute;

your self-atrocity condemned or repurposed –

a slow sinking of *The Bathhouse*,
the heart slow-sapping,

or for those in God's good management,
a sin that never ends
until warded off with prayer.

The facts dominate:

Russian Roulette
Twice victorious
Twice dead

A sharp grind to the skull,
A three-day pageant for the multi-thousands.

Vladimir, you are that which great minds have left behind –
precursory genius, a lisp in the ashes.

Vladimir, alas, your agonies, your theatre of nerves,
your 'jail of nights' for lack of a party card.

The gossip you'd hate,
as the dead undoubtedly do.

But time strikes late,
just past the hour – the 'Impossible',
in-leafed and yelling.

(Reverb) At the Scene of 'The Earthenware Head'

'The owl shall stoop down from his turret, the rat cry out'
Sylvia Plath, 'Watercolour of Grantchester Meadows'

Two strides from the Cam,
away from that pebbly grey town
to a crotched chestnut idly summering.

> Fenwork of rat and owl,
> two lovers nitching to a cross.

Steering horticulture she was,
your gifted watercolour of '59
framed, impure,
(if not for love) a mockery.

> No mythic shrine here.
> No stopped clock.

The mirrorbowl of the river
reflects on a loop:
resourceful antlers, black hedgerow,
arcades of sky.

But further, closer,
(detected through my own face)
no chapel service was ever held down there,

nothing but the pale conception in a dead syllable,
the ring of a widow who refused to marry well.

From a steep of moss,
I fork my hands into the greasy branches
for the orphaned head you looked for
in passing and in vain.

How hard did you stare?

In every easel,
(to be found out cunning)
she eulogised your step in the weather.

And you, ploppy water rat,
wished to know why it was placed here.

Prospecting Several Instances of Active Imagination

1   ('...who did you dream last night?')

Episodic, the spine: mother
as lunar sphinx. Her scent
Earth's unconsummated air.

Dragging behind her back
a ragdoll pulled along
by the roots of its ankle.

Nucleotidal, divided as woman /
mother. Her voice stammered
to embarrassed silence and... Cut.

*

The graininess: Super-8.
My double of five at the fair,
some inane shingled beach.

Beards of candyfloss at the pier.
Papa in his captain's uniform,
half his face pained with stroke,

half, as if happy. Good shipmate
the sea, his pallbearer, arranged
to take him out, as love had.

II   ('You shouted in your sleep, again…')

Electronically charged,
the street lines up
familiar and strange
the way animal is.

The sign over the ironmongers
pendulums to the mountain's degree,
it squeaks like a tree bucking.
I enter the house invisibly.

Honey-like, the ironmonger
grins, guarded by wasps.
He hisses to his protectorates
outjockeying mortality.

III   ('…like dying and feeling uncontrollably sick')

Studied Life at mother's school, one of her
boys cracked when roosting madness.

He whipped my pool cue to a spike,
stood there proud as a butcher.

Prime cut, a behavioural type,
I prepared my corpse for the jackal.

At forty feet my brother and father,
agoraphobics, shocked outdoors.

They touch for the first time in years
and fuse like a match to a cigarette.

IV   ('So, who is... *Soraya*?')

Devilled by a plush of lipstick.
She bled before even kissing.
Swaggerjack, feather in my mouth,
I was a crumb sweetening.

v   ('I was dreaming you...')

Safe-saddle to your crown,
these arms. The sun, a forefinger,
its print-run the cushioned field.

Light as anthem covering
cloud-baled mountains.
Chillon's miratorium in bloom.

On a column, under glass:
BYRON. Beside him, my scrawl:
'could not love then as I do here'.

51

Four Interpretations of Photographs by Claude Cahun

30o (Hand Trio)

The human hand gleams and imposes itself
cannily, like the white glove of SS Wolff.

If such configurations could rejoin the living,
Goebbels would be at the flashbulb, mad as a yapping seadog.

The black hand belonged to a spying washmaid in Nantes.
Any half-trained eye can see the curlicues.

Unbeknown to her – a '30s Telphousa –
she is grinding the wheelmill of war.

The baby hand is puppet-like and cut from the wrist.
Its cold digits are sized to the tip of an icicle.

Through the fingers of the child, darkness merges, entwists.
A blousy tablecloth rivers into ice, bloats to a hold, solid.

260 (Military Tailors)

Crocodilian wars where a sacred bull glints the shadow-stamp
of an 8-ball on his own forehead.

On conscripting, I was fitted up here.
Samuel & Finch. Haymarket. A three-piece. 1912.

It was the suit I pillowed my face into
fresh from Loos   crying:

God is not dead,
God wears the face of my enemy sleeping.

Entrenched   proceeding from dark to dark,
the early moon would watch back

doomy, unflinchingly alert,
like the skull of a pterodactyl.

44f (Self-Portrait Among Masks and a Crystal Skull)

i. Centremask –
Mutant Japanese. The disconnected neck round as the face of a
Bodhrán.

ii. Far Left Centremask –
Baselump of Marx's tomb. Blank eyeholes, the dunce-stare of
an age wasted.

iii. Upper Left Crystal Skull –
One thirteenth of world exposed. The ghost-luck beauty
fidgets in its glass.

iv. Self-Portrait –
Skeletal hermit, invisible until looked for. Wind-weary with a
Gestapo sneer.

v. Right Centremask –
Lunatic humiliated by ancestry. Hair pierced straight. Fraying
for lack of evidence.

35z (Flowerhead)

The seed of it   Hindu / Parisian –

not the blurry portico
but desire in the bangles of a bronze baroness,
a three-jet of pigeons –

the nine-blossoms of a head-flower
petrified, erect.

Scabbed wrists offer possibilities of self-portrait:

a young-un spaced clear, genderless
but for the touch of a nursery mother.

This is your mother.
Un-witched. Dregs of you.

Five Interpretations of Overpainted Photographs by Gerhard Richter

'8.4.89' (No Thing as Itself)

From the wakefulness of memory
the featliness of a grown wood – now

        tinctured by the tropics

        trochidae flatscreened
        to the tail of a lorikeet

*

I have returned to reinvent a life
that has germinated without me – now

        amnesia rattles in the firs

        The path more certain
        than the walk we made of it

'16.2.98' (Mother and Child, Sundown)

Carapace drapes the footer

      A mother's voice – natal oak –
      slides over her wet-headed child

  *

Marmoreal through an open room

      Poised – yet freeze-framed –
      for the branch to temper the leaf

'18.1.89' (Biogenesis)

Flesh over flesh
fated iron –

From the hanging distance
        of a whittled house

                white rain on chalklight

two honeymooners
        touched
        by the wing-spray of seraphs

    *

Brooded over for thirty years
the almanac sings

        You in your ivory wedding coat
        And I a ghoul in a funeral suit

'*11.1.89'* (On Brooke's Soldier)*

Some corner of a foreign field…
breakwater and a bowl of blood

*

Think only this of me…
Sweet courage among sandbanks

*

When the wind muscles up
the graves find new corpses

'23.2.96' (Items for Review)

A pool of sweat chills the floor

*

The summons of an unending corridor

*

A grasping of hands and legs

*

Spike-marks tacked to the wall

*

First killer against second killer

*

Put a flag in the room and watch it weep

Avoiding a Close Reading of Geoffrey Hill's
Mercian Hymns

Wind-flurried. Vicious martyrology.
So hints the robed guide to Mercia.
I underscratched the treasure-chest –

came back bald as a worn button.
What use in it all? History turned
into liquid? Tales of a money-king?

Seems the Midlands were variable.
Derby, all by itself, a tribal mansion.
You said the ivies were 'barbaric',

that trees buffed up like cutlery.
I underscore 'horned phonograph' with
'*Bullying. Mandarin.* Thank sticks!'

Sod the blimps. Loomis specked gold
onto gloomy shutters and you dived in
'to wash the wound that will not heal',

to stare hard over England's ashes.
I speculate on the finale. I suspect a kind
of mystic was involved. An elm witch.

There was a church dividing the road
triangularly. She had a magpie cackle.
With a poised, thistly face, she said:

Magic is for the staggeringly gifted.
The rest of us are furniture.
We move from room to room.

Three Presumptions whilst in the Neighbourhood of a Friend

for Niall McDevitt

The dying year is sentenced
to currency shackles, cruel alchemy.

On cobbled stone, savage trade –
windows of the Apollo mouth to mouth.

Here blood coils on a compass point.
Here to be mute is to gather seed.

*

You recall the face of Achamoth,
her pre-sculptural divinity.

For her you claimed a year of apotheosis,
leper-robed: wisdom your cure.

(But she was no Goddess. When we met
she took my hand like a scorpion.)

*

Over Furnival Gardens, onion light
pointillates the curve of the Thames.

From closed lawns of the Upper Mall,
through the needlehole of The Dove's alley,

a boy on his heels pulls the surface edge
as if he could peel a layer of glass.

Voice Portraits of Uncle Patrick at The Reunion House

Vulnerable, icy place The Beechwood –

bedworthy once,
now centuries of dovetail, lily-liver, brickbat.

Ossuary-toned,
pilestocked with Christmas port,
the old man,
his restive shrinery –

encores at Jimmy's Bar,
first loves carved into the Avocian font,
whisky-edits at the Lynhams of Laragh.

In St. Kevin's kitchen
no dignity there –

more a grumbly man who
puts it down to peckheaded women,
sharp air, 'a month of minor faults'.

(But in ruins, Uncle Pat.
Such a place to lose oneself!)

At the reunion
in his tasselled robes –

marriage as boarding house,
youth and its crime-scenes
miraculously transformed.

'During our engagement I inched along...
such determination,
the Jerry-boys called me *Hedgehog*'.

*

Behind the photo album,

spits over Battenberg.
Bruises necktied,
1951 in slings and braces.

*

The turning key of him,
exonerated,

as if he were preparing
for the mightiest of reunions:

his wife restored, unbroken.

'He paid fist-currencies.'

'His bovine grin stretched across the ballroom,'

'His body was loaded and tense'

'Such a life to struggle sober with.'

Not the Arm Wrestle

for Fiona Curran & Kurt MacDonald

Choose Kant agglutinated to a country field,
a stubborn lip to his stubborn mouth,
couched on the banks of the Pregolya.
His starting point: not the well-worn Eulerian path,
more earth suffering in its many vaults,
shook to the stem by Terrestrial Convulsions.

Choose Baudelaire, his treacherous god
the bordello, the bracken-shrink of childhood,
mother's clothes sleeping in a drawer like ivory.
Not the arm wrestle, your hoofy grin,
or the woman whose arm you snap back
hot with victory.

What makes the church-bell
a hideous sound from Lisbon to Paris?
For three days Kant wept inconsolably
as spires speared the pews on All Saints' Day,
crushed candles into fire, crushed a king,
crushed the tide so firmly it combusted,
roughhousing an entire city.

Unravel the plates of your tissue-thin armour,
there are stone blocks of history against which
to whiten a fist. Drink your gift 'Responsibly',
it is the finest full-bodied whisky in Europe.
Moths connoisseur for it, tremble at your glass.

The Angel vs. Gabriel

'Teach? It cannot be done.'

Ezra Pound, The Pisan Cantos *LXXIV*

My new student was pruneyarded into Creative Writing
for a shade of the family purse. He wants for his thesis
a re-launched critique of Mayakovsky's 'Cloud in Trousers'.

Gabriel, my student, like Mayakovsky, is deadly striking
and twenty-two, as was the poet when writing his tetraptych.
Yet he flounders at the notion that 'poets must tramp for days
with callused feet, and the sluggish fish of the imagination'.

I am irritable: a martyr to red tape: 'How will you write
even a preface on Mayakovksy without knowing the grotesque
alongside love and penury?' He was the nail in his boot,
he put his heart on the spit and, as in the Cloud, was swept
by the storm, trampled by the mad and clasticated by fire.

At present, Gabriel hasn't even the guts for the typing.
I can teach him nothing of inheritance above literature.

Inclub Satires

A Note to Ezra Pound from The Dreamer Party

Dear Loomis,

I, too, may risk Nimes to avoid the new Munros.

The whole night through,
Tiny-Tears in his gastric-sagging suit
skerrys about
molesting like a young rooster.

It makes me sick to the balls.

Shy at the pulpit,
the latest species (a cock-pheasant)
introduces then reintroduces the rooster,
who honours the applause with a pelvic wobble.

The Dreamer Prize
is little more than a vernal farce:

Brownload nods through it
like a loose button,
his burgundy lapel
dribble-stained –
clear evidence
he lost his wits in the 60s.

The poems are a death hand
that shint sideways
into what you have lettered:
malignant buncomb.

Everyone else appears
to appreciate the gyrator –
Zin-Zan smiles at his wife
as if he can see snow coming.

While the recently-queened Chanel Poet
(buffed up like a porcelain apple)
cares to market absolute clarity,
and so, says nothing of minor importance.

Lit. Fest. *(INSERT HERE)*

Holiness unhusked: elegise a losing mind
The idea arrives in language we don't understand

*

Spoilbank of domesticity, inspiration a spiderplot
It leapt up and said WRITE ME! A complete ambush

*

Banquet rooms spill with latent patronesses
Would you like to carry my Rilkeian sonnets?

*

A ferric weight makes anti-bubbles in the air
If I could island one word, 'delft' would be her

*

Institutional racism glossed over in the Q&A
Should have brought more than a shawl, m'duckie

*

Thunder aftergongs – Lightening butts the room
I have no idea – It just came to me – It was like dictation

Klepto

Translation for inside-leg   Careerism for inside-leg

    The thrill-hunt began on a Cantab lawn
    It will muzzle the divorce houses of Rabak

Translation as anaesthesia to war

Klepto – with hideous reptilian poise –
sneers at the provost

      enemious the faculty
      enemious the graduates

          Inside the funeral of her workshop
          the *taf'eelah* is serpented

'In a city of over 300 languages
few would suspect' –

      So masterous the breach
      it humiliates to a tinnitus of Roget

'The world owes enough to suit me' she says

the literals refurbished
plagiarised to murder –

'Akhawa' for 'Akhoya'
'Gamal' for 'Zina'

every posture in the text bifurcates

The Combover

A hard-boiled topper
oil-eaten,
slated sideways,
spaghetti-ing.

From my back-row vantage
a scandal of hair,
the cold smile
(seemingly immotile)
a jacklegger scotched
for milliseconds at a time.

Witness the shitting of vowels,
the convulsive flux,
the bronze eye,
those familiar orchestral gesturings
turning away
to thoughts of legacy.

King of the Stouts

Orion of Facebook   friends come clicking

For the famed nominee   floribundas of fan-mail

His success-theories   meet the world head-straight

Twizzle a duck-cane   the sightbeam of an eyetooth

*

Day-jobs   Drayhorse   Demulsifier

Stockpiler for *Riesling*   circus-master of Peking

For bellyrubs ebayed   via Chinese gossamers

Trivia-tested   the length of a grovet hold

*

Pssst-Coital   Sleuthhounded

Tell the boys   when she rides she rides

Like a Destrier   the pillow fat with hairsprings

Her hand in rolls   her wrists thin as baby clarinets

*

Savvy knight	Sword-featherer
Curatorial precision	serves life in the mirror
Scaremonger snout-nose	King of the Stouts
Your insignia	evidence precursors the crime

Acceptance Speech (with bracketed reverb)

'Aside from distinguished friends
my most calculable of judges

Aside from those who clutch
– as we must in these times –
the common candle

Aside from Larkin
his limpet-clinging proxy-squad

       (What we are is *movement* in a rapid world)

Aside from keen-eared mummy-bunnies
whose letters genuinely moved me
and perhaps – more tellingly –
moved my career to acceleration

Aside from the Chinese wine waiter
who turned into a tree
as – brainstoned by Christmas port –
I scoffed half the index of a menu

and young Jimmy   my prized student
who footed the bill
when I played hugger-mugger
and this ceremony last
shooed me from the stage in tears

(What we are is *movement* in a rapid world)

*

I dedicate this award to the English blackbird
the English hawthorn
the resilient cross of St. George

Bless these three rounds in a top hat and tails

This is for unmade murals in water
for cloud-vapours   surf-canons
freshets in false spring

*

We are Godless
our sins are unanswerable

What we are is *movement* in a rapid world.'

Double Dare

Our moon has the face of a gumlah;
it breeds like a horse. Neither do we fill or contain.

Raizella, leave the ologists faining over formulae.
Leave the Chinese zodiac to forensics and porcelain.

Stand in awe as the Kabuki players pack the stage
at Sadlers. Their tale, an old one: *The Purple Wisteria*.

It takes laws to encrypt the gestures of a hand.

Encore! (At the Request of Madame Hell)

'Simpkins, because my childhood is over
and I married the wrong kind, terribly young,

because there are not enough angels
in the New Testament and I struggle with tax-gravities,

recite for me again your grief-stained editor's poem,
the one that begins with Marxist traitors
and ends in cocktail pollution.

I am trenched in a battlefield of paperwork.
I am a descendent of Hegel and a Tory emblem.

Give me a single razorblade or a beauty mole.
I have the power to put you on a billboard,
to drink you by the neck, to swing doors.'

Doctor One-Eye

'...it is Heaven that has brought you here among us, my poor
child! Do you know that you have cost me...one eye...? What
a handsome shape is here! and what is this world!'
                Dr. Pangloss to Pacquette in Voltaire's *Candide*

The gas-blue iris   muddy in its architecture

A world where Balor re-emerges
        alone at Mag Mell
his incest armies
        struck with sea-vertigo

                    where Jacques the Anti-baptist
                        washes up in Peniche
                flush as a water emerald

and Cunegonde
        (for a chicken-coop of diamonds)
covers her kiss with a blush

        *

Prescripts of the One-Eye   its immaculate extensions

Dr. Pangloss   his future currencies   melancholia for profit

        Raynards   Beri-Beri   the Great Plagues

Here   death as the Big Dipper
                    the funeral carthorse
                    the stag staring into an empty well

82

*

Fifty years pivoting in the saddle
        for a surgery in Heakers

Trained on cardiacs   colics
        the Cushing egg dummy   the rubber hammer

This Panglossian   this over-achiever
        his cornea gleams like a clot of sputum

*

Before the slap of a Dunlop summons
        he is both legal
        and legally bound –

To the bad eye   blacklisters

Leibniz   Stalin   mac Lir

*

This *dark world*   where a red sheep becomes target board

Where Hookworm nemotodes are Epsomed in the windpipe

and tap-tappings of Thailidomide
        plump the foetus big as an Elstar

Inviting the Ghosts

Cemetery names for the newborn?

Fogel if a boy.
Ancora, a girl.

You've a wide claim to both:
the same hips as Cybil Shepherd
before she dropped Zachariah and Ariel.

Though the foetus
is small as a bowl of rice,
you create instances;

the triumphant darling
carried to your mother's farmhouse
over a harp-shaped lake;

a dollface, bewildered by motherese,
engineering a way to outwit
the entire family:

six centuries of violence.

Thieves' Society

Brooding as killable. The corner Joe in his goldfish globe sings
Venus. Doom-weighty in blue casuals. Tail-up. Clocky. A magpie
on the pounce. Fan-collared. Tightly-buckled. Teeth in a jig.

*

Hobbling between blackouts, the local Henne, local paw-bearer:
her bones and belly protruding for a pinch with the matricide.
The works for a monkey, trussed in the dark like a caught fish.

*

Bureaus of exile and immigration. New Herods in army fatigues.
A gang of ragpickers oil-faced over drumfire, their blue mouths
split open. All night, the severed bell. The whipcrack of boxcars.

*

In Garry bars the once-ambrosial. Rounds of Happyslap. Hophead.
Stick the gullet blade. Two taps to bald the face of a kitchen window.
The boiler suit fits all. The foursquare room with a chain-bit libbard.

*

On the lower delta: slickbacks, cockroaches drunk on their own sweat.
Washboard tenements where the old play Gin. Turn to Saigon, Hanoi.
News of the Imperial Tower looted. Trees peeled for coffins, crucifixes.

To-tock-ah-noo-lah, Yosemite National Park

The push-hand of To-Tock (Big Chief)
timetames from a cretaceous world.

Flathead of Merced's ice beaker,
who cracked on being born an orphan –
drowned old, rose young again,
glaciated at 3,593 ft., to profit beauty.

Human births are ignorant,
they are perishable, single-seeded.

On arriving at his own birth,
To-Tock was pitted by rocking tides
for .3 million years.

To the Ahwahneechee,
deep in unmarked, bouldered graves,
he must have seemed honeytrapped
when caught by the missionaries –
a giant Holofernes head, dispirited
but for stubbornness so tall it's starpinned.

*

Tourists stamp ice at The Happy Isles,
plough snowchains through Curry Village –
their sleek SUV's charioteered
by lumberjacks tracking a circular route,
a view restocked via digital memory.

I, too, uncapped the lens, tried to button tight
live signpostings to a Kavan scene.
The vision failed flatteringly.

Up close to the eye, in XXL format,
astonished cinema, societies of ice
crusted into the world's greatest monolith.

At the root of its navigable Nose,
the veins are gracile, tri-granular,
peeled bald to obstinacies rooted
at 100 mya or more.

To front here
human is houndbitch, at best
a pearl of grammar, a green stare
from the activist who stands back
awkward as Fuseli's self-portrait.

                *

At ground level to 260 feet:
Sequoiadendron giganteum.

Scouring the route of the Mariposa valley,
To-Tock might spy her as a warning sign –
a forced cross on this sacred battlefield,
midget shinbone to an underworld of ice.

On Not Reaching a Summit

Charcoal smudges where runways stood
roll towards the suburban hells.

Across the cracked sieve of wheatfields,
clouds plash a diagonal rain.

At the liquid border, in blonde smoke:
unmanned ships, masts like a hand drowning.

A crow was the first to evacuate. His loot:
a rat ripped clean out of its fur.

A fox followed with a chill in its throat
and the stars gave up their hardbreathing.

In a shadow of crosses, a priest sits alone,
peeling his robes with a knife.

A Room in the House of Aries

Inside the fire-house
a waking taste of basalt grain,
monstrance of the raven
cindering a jewel in its mouth.

To wake here is to salute
the memory of fire.
I held an apple from my father.
It was burnt black to the seed.

'Come now', she said,
'carry the weight of your life.'
The surgeon fixed his knife
and the moon rose as witness.

Dragon Tree

for Sandeep

The blue-rimmed room
distinguishably yours

a weeklong lingering
jasmine tinged with pomegranate

Dry meat
I lay down my limbs for you

and with an armful of pillow
I study your note
its weaponry –

life over death
and distance that can be narrowed
to the length of a finger

All night a lute-wind
your Dragon Tree
nods through the dark

shivering to keep green
its tens and twenties

Incest

The only sound is recorded rain.
It's the kind insomniacs buy on CD:
a sound so tight it's almost syllabic.

The camera goes in on Francine.
The low-cut hoop of her blue hem
billows up from the wind machine.

The cold makes two round stings
of her nipples. The director looks
keen and terrified, but keeps it rolling.

His lead walks in and fluffs the line.
With her he can only play himself:
a version of the sea, uncontainable.

Their strange breed of surface tension
is capable of locking a bedroom door.
The villain is a ghost in white sheets.

Jackanoria

My grandmother's nightstories
held together by an odour of blood.
Her oceans were flaked with silver,
clear moons ghosted in the reeds.

Plotlines were a speciality, worlds
crammed with backstairs influence,
the all-knowingness of elf maidens,
a blue dragon coasting through twilight.

With eyes bulbous and widening,
she warned of stone-hearted pirates,
of pilfering doxies, of glass-green
witches gossiping in their hags.

Her damsel would arrive tear-tender
and unmistakably cursed, always
cast as the one pure virgin and made
from the dust of a thousand heavens.

The hero, a grown-up version of myself,
(though twice the mutineer and poor
as a housefly) carried his sacrifice
blindly, for love among the ruins.

Entry (Cornwall 1991)

You never saw how her eyes attempted to recite the explosive
    wings of birds.
Or how, as rain swept in off the desolate coast, willing its
    improbable magnetics,
her ringless finger would mark the threat of clouds, pointing
    itself to the sky
defiantly like a spire. Perhaps it was for the best, for as she
    scaled the rocks like that,
arms spread like a Celtic cross, truly, you would have loved her.

A Local Marriage

The rodo bride waits for ultrasound.

Her childhood's worth of jealousies,
tight as honeycomb,
hardly vocable.

From his front stall
the father of the bride plays Marketplace,
Beg for a Diamond, Old Man's Eye –

his Buddha smile
latticework for a wife,
she, too, corona-red and local,
as if the family blood depended on it.

*

The groom is aristocratically-nosed
and finely dieted –
a muscled swimmer
if the arms dictate anything.

(Not exactly a temple fit for Samson,
but in these villages
small blessings are capable of tracery
and can make for a healthy platter.)

Napoleon-like in these parts,
whilst still only twenty-six,

his father's father's wharf-pile of riches
count double (once inherited).

A man raised by the whip
truly scienced,
with the memory of an elephant –

stag nights at la Coahuila,
fistfights in El Paso, love
as Shelly championed it...

All in a gentleman's education!

The Ashes

Who knows what has become of him –
the mad bastard. But I sense he's at it,
prowling the backrooms of dive-bars,
as if stuck in a labyrinth. With the same
not-to-be-trusted look, the same smile,
readable to anyone in the entire room
that says how tonight is not merely
an episode in his life, but moreover,
that here is a man who would sell
some of his own organs for a nightcap.
He'll be carrying two brandies back
from the bar, shuffling along
in that way of his, as if he were trying
to walk a line of string. Or court-jesterly
at The Troy, telling long tales like how
he survived three weeks on a mountain
in Tibet on nothing but tea and cigarettes.
Or my favourite story, if only for the way
he would tell it, the one that ended
a week after the cremation of his Pa,
when, as he sat there, striving to mourn,
the urn suddenly fell from the mantelpiece
and he scooped up a handful of the ashes
to wash down his father with a chase of Bells.

The Minister's Daughter

In the heat-wave of '91
no one suspected a thing.
Your father (who worked
vigorously for Our Father)
would return from the ministry
in his clapped-out Renault,
and we'd hear it crunching
up the gravel fifty yards away.

Perfecting the routine
we'd already talked through,
you'd leap upright from the bed
and wheel around the room,
snatching up garments
until your naked body
was clad in something
that suggested innocence.

From the dusty hideaway
of your double wardrobe,
I'd hear the front door clack,
listen for the scuff of his shoes
and mark the shy animal
in your voice as you offered
a fresh brew or asked questions
about the congregation.

Sometimes I'd wait an age,
acclimatise to the shadows
and think of that old wardrobe
as a strange kind of seclusion,
like that of a confessional booth.
I'd confess my sins to the dark
still aroused amid the hangings
of your silk summer dresses.

What Remains of Old Addresses

'Thus the whole thing is scattered about inside me, the rooms,
the stairs that descended with such ceremonious slowness,
others narrow cages that mounted in a spiral movement, in
the darkness of which we advanced like the blood in our veins'.
Rainer Maria Rilke, *Notebooks of Malte Laurids Brigge*

The Nook

The musty smell of Barbour jackets
slung lazily over the coat stand.
A pungency of something resembling
cabbage water from the net-curtains,
and wardrobes like a sandy shelf
of old paperbacks. The stairs climb
until out of reach. A loose plank
lifts from the top step; if scaled
it would feel so cold to the touch.
Up there, a mother coo-coos at a child
to stifle its cries. The noises compete
and grow into a kind of turbulence.
The door opens. Light pours in.
A kettle pipes fiercely in the kitchen.

Kajati

In the garden, at its furthest point
from the bungalow, where sunlight
twitches between the cherry trees,
the lawn becomes uneven, rutted
from where a child had once spent

hours turning his fingers in the soil.
And now, standing at the same point,
if you dig far enough under the earth
you'll discover what was left there:
an old wooden pencil-box that opens
to the smell of carnations and rain.
And inside you'll find a photograph,
slightly foxed, of a young couple
beside a lake: a conventional scene.

Ferncroft

Red letters wedged under the door,
too many for counting, all addressed
to the man who vanished one night
into a blue winter fog. One year on,
above the hush, a workaholic ghost
taps Morse-like on the blinds.
And a sound, like the grinding of knives,
quickens faintly from the kitchen.
Potential tenants pace about the house
stopping at the bedroom door.
They notice the chill of the room
and gawp down at the bed in confusion
as if it were the hub of a crime scene
and lacked only a death, a body.

Holly Mansions

Three months into my tenancy here
and the landlord mentions a young girl,
Chloe, who went mad in the bedroom.
As he tells it, three men in white smocks
charged in to find her blood-splashed,
and sure a devil was rustling in the loft.
Every time he comes for the money,
my landlord offers no explanation
for her madness. But six months in
and I have begun to feel a little closer
to what it was: the menacing white
of the walls in winter, the way faces
shapeshift in knots of the wardrobe.
I wake to the dark, thinking of her.

Testimony

While others looked on you as scenery and called your name
through bile and blood, I remained silent and in doing so
I've kept my promises. This is evidence, real as a gold piece.
I was your pallbearer; I held the weight of your life in my arms.

Notes

p. 10 'Apprentice Work': The poem references the work of Peter Redgrove, including titles of his own poems, such as 'The Gale Chambers of the Vast Nose' (published in *A Speaker for the Silver Goddess*, Stride, 2006).

p. 12 'Air Terminals': Quotes have been taken from Katherine Mansfield's short story 'A Cup of Tea'. 'Rosemary' refers to the principal character in the story.

p. 15 'Days of 1973': 'The kettle yearns for the mountain / The soap for the sea' is a quote from the Derek Mahon poem 'Nostalgia'.

p. 21 'Sestina for R': The repeated and part-repeated lines of Edna St. Vincent Millay ('Like a vessel too thin / For certain vibrations.') are from the poem sequence 'Ragged Island' and taken from the posthumous collection, *Mine the Harvest* (published by Harper & Brothers, 1954).

The Brain was a 'Rave' club at 11, Wardour Street, Soho, London between 1990-1992.

p. 28 'Two Phonecalls at 4 am': All 'anecdotes' relating to Li Po are fictitious.

p. 35 'Serapis from a Postcard': Serapis was a syncretic Hellenistic-Egyptian god. He was 'invented' by Ptolemy Soter.

p. 37 'The Buddhas of Bamiyan': Among the tallest and oldest in the world, the Buddhas of Bamiyan were destroyed by the Taliban in 2001 because they were thought to be 'against Islam'. 54 member states of the Organisation of the Islamic Conference (OIC) protested before the monuments were destroyed. Dr. Tarzi believes that a previously unidentified Buddha (1000 ft. in height) is under the rubble at Bamiyan. He is still digging to unearth it.

p. 41 'Chess in Kirkuk': Al-Mutanabbi (915-965) (full name Abu at-Tayyib Ahmad ibn Huseyn Al Mutanabbi), was an Iraqi-born poet. He is regarded as one of the greatest poets in the Arabic language. His flair for satire may have also been one of the reasons for his death. When travelling to Kufah in September 965, he was supposedly killed by the chief of a tribe he had insulted. Al-Mutanabbi can be loosely translated as 'he who claims to be a prophet'.

p. 43 'Sanchez de Aldama': 'llello' is a Cuban-Spanish slang term for cocaine.

A 'cochinita' is a baby pig, commonly roasted for cochinita pibil, a Mexican dish from Yucatán.

p. 45 '14th April 1930': On his death, Vladimir Mayakovsky's brain was surgically removed by the 'State Institute for the Study of the Brain' and taken to the Institute's Pantheon. Approximately 150,000 people came to view Mayakovsky's body 'as it lay in state at the Club of the Writer's Federation, under a wreath made of hammers, flywheels and screws'.

p. 49 'Prospecting Several Instances of Active Imagination': Active imagination was developed by C. G. Jung. It is a meditation technique often used to translate emotions into images or narratives and can serve as a bridge between the conscious self and the unconscious, which includes working with dreams and the creative self via imagination or fantasy. In conceiving of the idea Jung wrote: 'I was sitting at my desk once more, thinking over my fears. Then I let myself drop. Suddenly it was as though the ground literally gave way beneath my feet, and I plunged into the dark depths.'

The final stanza of the last movement of the poem refers to Lord Byron's hand-carved signature on a pillar of the Chateau de Chillon, Montreux, Switzerland.

p. 52 'Four Interpretations of Photos by Claude Cahun': Championed by André Breton in her early career – but eventually considered 'too surreal for the Surrealists' – Claude Cahun (b. 1894) was a French photographer, artist, poet and political activist who lived with her half-sister Suzanne Malherbe in Paris and in Jersey, where they lived from 1937. When the Nazis occupied Jersey during World War II, Cahun and Malherbe joined the resistance and produced anti-German propaganda fliers, which were disseminated at Nazi meetings, with Cahun often disguised in German soldier's uniform. In 1944 both women were arrested and sentenced to death. Although these sentences were never carried out, Cahun suffered greatly from respiratory problems after her release, which led to a premature death in 1954.

The title codes included in this poem are the original identities from Cahun's negatives, as part of the exhibition at Camden Arts Centre, 'Strange Events Permit Themselves the Luxury of Occurring' (December 2007-February 2008.) Bracketed titles are the author's own.

p. 56 'Five Interpretations of Overpainted Photographs by Gerhard Richter': The dates in the titles are Gerhard Richter's own titles. The bracketed titles are the authors.

p. 63 'Three Presumptions Whilst in the Neighbourhood of a Friend: 'Achamoth' in Gnostic texts refers to the name of a lower Sophia. Esoterically, and with the Gnostics, the elder Sophia was the Holy Spirit (female Holy Ghost) or the Sakti of the Unknown, and the Divine Spirit. Sophia Achamoth is the personification of the female aspect of the creative male force in nature, or astral light.

p. 65 'Voice Portraits of Uncle Patrick at The Reunion House': The third to fifth stanzas, in the first movement of the poem, include names of various places or people from County Wicklow, Ireland, such as Saint Kevin of Glendalough.

p. 68 'Not the Arm Wrestle': Immanuel Kant was born in Königsberg, which is at the mouth of the Pregolya River. Shocked at the devastation of the Lisbon earthquake of 1755, he published three separate books based on his studies of the tragedy, which was estimated to have killed between 10,000-100,000 people.

p. 82 'Doctor One-Eye': The poem references central characters in Voltaire's *Candide*, and plays on the Leibnizian mantra of Dr. Pangloss: 'all is for the best in the best of all possible worlds'. It also recalls the scandalous misuse of the drug Thalidomide, which was prescribed during the late 1950s and early 1960s to pregnant women, to deal with symptoms of childbirth, including morning sickness. Before its release, inadequate tests were performed to assess the drug's safety. Between 1956-62 approximately 10,000 children were born with severe birth defects as a result of their mothers having been prescribed the drug.

Balor, according to Celtic mythology, was the one-eyed king of the Fomorians – a giant, semi-divine race who ruled Ireland in ancient times. It was said his one eye could kill anyone it looked upon.

'Dunlop summons' refers to the findings of the Committee for the Safety of Medicines, set up by Sir Derek Dunlop. The Committee's research into the dangers of medical prescription resulted in the Medicines Act of 1968.

An Elstar is an apple from the Golden Delicious family.

p. 86 'To-tock-ah-noo-lah': The Ahwahneechee people lived in California's Yosemite Valley approximately 800 to 1000 years ago.

Biographical Note

JAMES BYRNE was born in Buckinghamshire in 1977 and divides his time between New York City and London. He is Editor of *The Wolf*, a poetry magazine he co-founded in 2002. His debut collection, *Passages of Time*, was published by Flipped Eye in 2003. He has translated the Yemeni national anthem and is currently working on a project to publish contemporary Burmese poets. In 2008, he won the Treci Trg Poetry Festival prize in Serbia. In 2009 his *New and Selected Poems: The Vanishing House* was published by Treci Trg (in a bilingual edition) in Belgrade. In 2009 his poems were translated into Arabic for the Al-Sendian Cultural Festival in Syria. He is the co-editor of *Voice Recognition: 21 Poets for the 21st Century*, published by Bloodaxe, and is co-editing *Paris and Other Poems* by Hope Mirrlees (Fyfield Books 2011).